Dedi

MW01600678

I dedicate this book to my Momma Sharon Sharp, who planted seeds of the Word into my life since I was a little girl, who wanted everyone to know who Jesus is, and that everyone deserved forgiveness. She loved her kids, grandkids, and great grandkids with all her heart.

Romans 10:9
That if you confess with your mouth the Lord Jesus and believe in your heart that God has raised Him from the dead, you will be saved.

Prayer of Salvation:
"Lord Jesus, I repent of my sins and surrender my life. Wash me clean. I believe that Jesus Christ is the Son of God. That he died on the cross for my sins and rose again on the third day for my Victory, I believe that in my heart and make confession with my mouth, that Jesus is my Savior and Lord. Amen

Week One

Day 1
Joshua 1:8
8 Keep this Book of the Law always on your lips; meditate on it day and night, so that you may be careful to do everything written in it. Then you will be prosperous and successful.

Prayer:
Father God, as I take this Journey of Praying according to your Word, I will learn to meditate on the given scripture throughout the day. I believe that by doing this I am sowing the Word in my heart, and I will be prosperous and have good success. Amen

Journal / Notes:
This portion of scripture is encouraging us to meditate on the Word and to do according to what we learn. To meditate something is to "think deeply or carefully about "

Day 2
Galatians 6:7&8
7 Be not deceived; God is not mocked: for whatsoever a man soweth, that shall he also reap.
8 For he that soweth to his flesh shall of the flesh reap corruption; but he that soweth to the Spirit shall of the Spirit reap life everlasting.

Prayer
Father God, today I focus on this scripture knowing that I have a choice of what I am sowing in my life, that I will reap a harvest of your Word sown in my heart. I choose to sow to the Spirit by being faithful to meditate & pray according to your Word. Amen

Journal / Notes:
God loves us so much He gives us a choice; we choose what we sow in our life. Regardless of good seed or bad seed it will reap a harvest.

Day 3

1 Peter 5:6-7

Be humble in the presence of God's mighty power, and he will honor you when the time comes. God cares for you, so turn all your worries over to him.

Prayer:
Father God, I humble myself before you casting all my cares over to you just as the scripture says to do. I know that you care for me, I know that you see the obstacles in my life. Today and every day I will practice casting all my cares over to you and from this day forward I have no worries. Amen

Journal/ Notes:
We can live a carefree life as we continue to turn all of our cares (anxiety) over to God. He cares for us, and He wants to honor us.

Day 4

Matthew 6:26
Look at the birds of the air: they neither sow nor reap nor gather into barns, and yet your heavenly Father feeds them. Are you not of more value than they?

Prayer:
Father God, I come before you with the realization of how valuable I am as your child. You take care of the Birds of the air! How much more then you will provide for me! I rely on you Lord for provision. Amen

Journal / Notes:
We can rely on God to take care of us! We are much more valuable to Him then the Birds are, If He provides for them then I know He will provide for me.

Day 5

Matthew 6:33
Seek the Kingdom of God above all else, and live righteously, and he will give you everything you need.

Prayer:
Father God in the name of Jesus I pray that you guide me and teach me to put you first in all things. I want to do as the scripture says and "seek first the kingdom of God". I want to live righteously before you Lord. I know that you will give me everything that I need to do that, I know that I can find what I need in your Word. Thank you, Father! Amen

Journal / Notes:
The Kingdom of God is within us! As we put Gods Word first in our life by meditating His Word, Praying His Word and sowing it into our heart, it is then that we are seeking His Kingdom first.

Day 6

1 John 4:4
Ye are of God, little children, and have overcome them: because greater is he that is in you, than he that is in the world.

Prayer:
Father God, I thank you that You are greater in me then he that is in the World. This scripture brings me confidence that you are bigger than all the obstacles that come against me, that I can stand in Faith knowing that you are greater than all of them. Amen

Journal / Notes:
Just knowing that the greater one lives inside of me keeps me assured that I always walk in Victory!

Day 7

Joshua 1:8
8 Keep this Book of the Law always on your lips; meditate on it day and night, so that you may be careful to do everything written in it. Then you will be prosperous and successful.

Galatians 6:7&8
7 Be not deceived; God is not mocked: for whatsoever a man soweth, that shall he also reap.
8 For he that soweth to his flesh shall of the flesh reap corruption; but he that soweth to the Spirit shall of the Spirit reap life everlasting.

1 Peter 5:6-7
6 Be humble in the presence of God's mighty power, and he will honor you when the time comes. 7 God cares for you, so turn all your worries over to him.

Matthew 6:26
Look at the birds of the air: they neither sow nor reap nor gather into barns, and yet your heavenly Father feeds them. Are you not of more value than they?

Matthew 6:33
Seek the Kingdom of God more than
anything else, and live righteously, and he
will give you everything you need.

1 John 4:4
Ye are of God, little children, and have
overcome them: because greater is he
that is in you, than he that is in the world.

This week's Prayer according to the Word:

Father God as I have sown the seed of your Word into my life this week, I pray that it takes root and grows, that I reap a harvest of your Word in my life. I know that as I seek first the Kingdom of God and your righteousness that all things will be added unto me. I know that your word says that I am much more valuable than the birds of the air, you provide for them what they need, I know beyond any doubt that you will provide for me! Father God, I thank you that I can cast all my cares over to you, it frees me to focus more on you and continually giving you thanksgiving and praise! As I meditate on your Word throughout the week, I know in my heart that I will prosper and have good success according to your Word. Father, I continue to praise you for me being and overcomer because greater is He that is in me than He that is in the world.   Amen

Week Two

Day 1

2 Corinthians 10:3-5

For though we walk in the flesh, we do not war according to the flesh. For the weapons of our warfare are not carnal but mighty in God for pulling down strongholds, casting down arguments and every high thing that exalts itself against the knowledge of God, bringing every thought into captivity to the obedience of Christ.

Prayer:

Father God, Your Word says to cast down all imaginations that are not of you! Lord, I thank you that I do not have to entertain those thoughts, I thank you that I am able to keep my thoughts on you Lord. I bring those thoughts into captivity and set my mind on the things of you God. Amen

Journal / Notes

I have the mind of Christ and I don't have to dwell on things that do not honor God!

Day 2

Colossians 3:2
Set your mind on things above, not on things on the earth.

Prayer:

Father God thank you for direction in your Word, as I move forward in committing myself to praying your Word, I can also focus on walking these things out in my life. I will set my mind on things above; I will keep my eyes on you Lord Amen

Journal / Notes

Keeping our mind on the Word Daily, praying the scriptures is keeping focus on things above.

Day 3

Romans 12:2
Do not be conformed to this world but be transformed by the renewal of your mind, that you may prove what is the will of God, what is good, acceptable, and perfect.

Prayer:
Heavenly Father, I thank you that I have opportunity to renew my mind with your Word. I continue to read, speak, and pray your word so, that my mind will be renewed. In doing this I will be able prove what your will is Lord and see what is good, acceptable, and perfect! Amen

Journal / Notes

Read slowly: Take your time to understand the meaning of each word. Meditate: Dwell on interesting passages and think about them. Pray: Ask the Holy Spirit to help you believe what you read and apply it to your life. Memorize: Fill your mind with the word of God through memorization. Speak out loud: Think in a way that pleases God by speaking out loud or singing.

Day 4

Philippians 4:8

Finally, brethren, whatever things are true, whatever things are noble, whatever things are just, whatever things are pure, whatever things are lovely, whatever things are of good report, if there is any virtue and if there is anything praiseworthy—meditate on these things.

Prayer:

Father God, I honor your Word, I am willing meditate on things that are true, noble, just, pure, lovely and of good report. I will continue to praise you throughout the day and do it with Virtue. Amen

Journal / Notes

Virtue: setting these things as a high standard.

Day 5

Proverbs 4:20-22

My son, give attention to my words.
Incline your ear to my sayings. Do not let
them depart from your eyes; Keep them in
the midst of your heart; For they are life to
those who find them, And health to all
their flesh.

Prayer:
Thank you, God, for all your instruction
that you give me in your Word. I will give
attention to your Words and will incline my
ears to what you are saying to me, I will
not let them depart from my eyes and will
keep them in the midst of my heart. Thank
you for life and health. Amen

Journal / Notes
Keeping Gods word with us all the time
through meditation, will make impressions
on our heart, the promise is life and
health.

Day 6

Psalm 1:1-3
Blessed is the man that walketh not in the counsel of the ungodly, nor standeth in the way of sinners, nor sitteth in the seat of the scornful. But his delight is in the law of the Lord; and in his law doth he meditate day and night. And he shall be like a tree planted by the rivers of water, that bringeth forth his fruit in his season; his leaf also shall not wither; and whatsoever he doeth shall prosper.

Prayer:
God, I know that according to this scripture you are instructing me to not get worldly counsel, hang out with sinners or people that are rude, and lack respect but, instead delight myself in you and meditate on your Word Day and night, you promise that I will grow and bring forth fruit and prosper. I continue to commit my ways to you Lord. Amen.

Journal / Notes
I delight myself in the Lord for He is good; I prosper and am Fruitful just as he promises me!

Day 7

2 Corinthians 10:3-5
For though we walk in the flesh, we do not war according to the flesh. For the weapons of our warfare are not carnal but mighty in God for pulling down strongholds, casting down arguments and every high thing that exalts itself against the knowledge of God, bringing every thought into captivity to the obedience of Christ.

Colossians 3:2
Set your mind on things above, not on things on the earth.

Romans 12:2
Do not be conformed to this world but be transformed by the renewal of your mind, that you may prove what is the will of God, what is good, acceptable, and perfect.

Philippians 4:8

Finally, brethren, whatever things are true, whatever things are noble, whatever things are just, whatever things are pure, whatever things are lovely, whatever things are of good report, if there is any virtue and if there is anything praiseworthy—meditate on these things.

Proverbs 4:20-22
My son, give attention to my words. Incline your ear to my sayings. Do not let them depart from your eyes; Keep them in the midst of your heart; For they are life to those who find them, And health to all their flesh.

Psalm 1:1-3
Blessed is the man that walketh not in the counsel of the ungodly, nor standeth in the way of sinners, nor sitteth in the seat of the scornful. But his delight is in the law of the Lord; and in his law doth he meditate day and night. And he shall be like a tree planted by the rivers of water, that bringeth forth his fruit in his season; his leaf also shall not wither; and whatsoever he doeth shall prosper.

This week's prayer according to the Word:

Father God, You Lord are worthy to be praised! I honor you and worship you Father! This week has been about renewing my mind, casting down all imagination that exalt itself against you, be mindful of who I sit with and what I am keeping my mind on. This week's instructions promise fruitfulness, life and health. You are amazing God and faithful, you give me everything I need to proper, I will listen to the instruction in your Word, keep your Word close to my heart, in these instructions that you give me Lord I know that I will find your will for my life! Amen

Journal / Notes:

God gives us specific instruction in His Word all throughout the Bible, key take away this week> is our mind! Who we are representing by what we are focusing on. Who are we sitting with or getting our counsel from? Let it come from the Word of God not the world. Our warfare is in our mind! Renew it with the word of God and heed its instruction keeping it close to our heart. We will be fruitful and prosper.

Week 3

Day 1

Hosea 4:6

My people are destroyed for lack of knowledge: because thou hast rejected knowledge, I will also reject thee, that thou shalt be no priest to me: seeing thou hast forgotten the law of thy God, I will also forget thy children.

Prayer:

Father God your Word says that your people are destroyed for the lack of knowledge, thank you God that through Prayer, reading and meditating on your Word I grow in the knowledge of you! Who I am in Christ and what belongs to me as your child. Amen

Journal Notes:

I am full of knowledge of Gods Word as I continue in diligent time in meditating the Word of God.

Day 2

John 17:17

Sanctify them through thy truth: thy word
is truth.

Prayer:

Lord God! Thank you for your Word! Your
Word is Truth! I am sanctified by it! I am
full of Joy knowing that I can stand on
your Word and whatever it says I can do, I
can do, what ever it says that I can have, I
can have, and whatever it says that I am,
I am ! Amen

Journal / Notes:

I am washed with the Word!

Sanctify = set apart as or declare holy;
consecrate! free from sin; purify.

Day 3

1 Peter 2:9

But you are a chosen people, a royal priesthood, a holy nation, God's special possession, that you may declare the praises of him who called you out of darkness into his wonderful light.

Prayer:

Yes Lord, I am of a Holy Priesthood, a holy nation! I am a Special possession. Yes, God I give you all the Glory Honor and Praise, I thank you For bringing me out of the darkness and into the Wonderful Light! I am called by you God! Thank you, Lord! Amen

Journal / Notes:

So much to praise God for! He has brought us out of darkness! We are of a Royal Priest Hood! We are of a Holy Nation! We are hand picked by God, Special Possession!

Day 4

2 Chronicles 7:14

If my people who are called by my name
humble themselves, and pray and seek my
face, and turn from their wicked ways,
then I will hear from heaven, and will
forgive their sin and heal their land.

Prayer:

Holy Spirit, I pray that you keep me
Humble. Father God, I pray and seek your
face continually, I turn from sin and
humble myself before you God. Giving you
thanks always for who you are and what
you have done for me. I give you praise
Lord, thank you for healing our land! Amen

Journal / Notes:

Staying humble before God, continue to
pray and seek His face continually! Healing
is ours !

Day 5

John 14:27

Peace, I leave with you; my peace I give to you; not as the world gives do I give to you. Let not your hearts be troubled, neither let them be afraid.

Prayer:

Thank you God for Peace, a peace that I can't find anywhere other then you Lord! I know God, that you are the only way to true peace. I am not afraid Lord, and I am not troubled. Amen

Journal / Notes:

We can search everywhere and in everything to try and find peace although, any peace that we find other then God is a counterfeit, and it won't satisfy. Music (that perfect song) another person(soul mate) material things , money,. It will fail us and we will never experience true peace in those things.

Day 6

Philippians 4:7

Then, because you belong to Christ Jesus, God will bless you with peace that no one can completely understand. And this peace will control the way you think and feel.

Prayer:

Heavenly Father, your Word teaches that I am blessed with a peace that no one can completely understand because I belong to Christ Jesus and that this peace will control the way I think and feel. Thank you, God, that you have given me this peace that surpasses all understanding.

Journal / Notes:

Because of this Peace we can be calm in our thinking and how we feel, we do not have to be bound to the fast pace and pressures of this world .

Day 7

Hosea 4:6

My people are destroyed for lack of knowledge: because thou hast rejected knowledge, I will also reject thee, that thou shalt be no priest to me: seeing thou hast forgotten the law of thy God, I will also forget thy children.

John 17:17

Sanctify them through thy truth: thy word is truth.

1 Peter 2:9

But you are a chosen people, a royal priesthood, a holy nation, God's special possession, that you may declare the praises of him who called you out of darkness into his wonderful light.

2 Chronicles 7:14

If my people who are called by my name humble themselves, and pray and seek my face, and turn from their wicked ways, then I will hear from heaven, and will forgive their sin and heal their land.

John 14:27

Peace, I leave with you; my peace I give to you; not as the world gives do I give to you. Let not your hearts be troubled, neither let them be afraid.

Philippians 4:7

Then, because you belong to Christ Jesus, God will bless you with peace that no one can completely understand. And this peace will control the way you think and feel.

This week's prayer according to the Word

Father God, I humble myself before you God, bringing my mind will and emotions into submission before you! Praising you for all that you have given me and recognizing that I am of a Royal Priest Hood! I am of a chosen generation, I am your special possession, you have called me out of darkness! You have given me a peace that passes all understanding, a peace that only you can give. I thank you God that as I am diligent in prayer and meditation of your Word that I grow in the knowledge of it and sanctified by the truth of your word. Thank you for peace of mind that you have given me, for calling me out of darkness, I honor you, Lord! Amen

Week Four

Day 1

2 Corinthians 4:18

While we do not look at the things which are seen, but at the things which are not seen. For the things which are seen are temporary, but the things which are not seen are eternal.

Prayer:

Father God, I thank you that I don't have to be controlled by my circumstances. I thank you Lord that in the mist of all that try and oppose me I can stand on your Word which is eternal, Stand in Faith which is eternal. I know that the things I can see are only temporary and that you are forever! Amen

Journal / Notes:
I am controlled by the Word of God not circumstances or obstacles.

Day 2

Isaiah 54:17   CEV translation

Weapons made to attack you
    won't be successful;
words spoken against you
    won't hurt at all
My servants, Jerusalem is yours!
I, the Lord, promise
    to bless you with victory.

Prayer:

Thank you, Father, that no weapon that is
formed against me shall prosper and those
who rise against me will fall, this is a
promise to me that I stand on! Amen

Journal / Notes

No need to go into detail in our prayer
about all the things that we don't want to
happen or that we try and come against.
Keep it simple according to the word.
No Weapon will come against me.

Day 3

Psalms 23:4

I may walk through valleys
as dark as death,
    but I won't be afraid.
You are with me,
and your shepherd's rod
    makes me feel safe.

Prayer:

Thank you, God, that I do not have to fear
anything, that you make me feel safe and
that you are with me. I know there is
much evil around me but, it can't touch me
or harm me. Amen

Journal / Notes:

No matter what evil is around me in this
world it can't harm me or touch me unless
I allow it. Fear is not of God and it is tool
of evil, rest in the Word.

Day 4

1 Peter 1:5

You have faith in God, whose power will protect you until the last day. Then he will save you, just as he has always planned to do.

Prayer:

I keep my faith in you Lord for your promises are good. Your Word says that you will protect me until the end. I believe and trust in your Word and rest in knowing that you protect me.

Journal / Notes:

We are kept by the power of God through faith. Rely on Gods keeping power. When everything around me is crashing I am kept by Gods keeping power.

Day 5

Ephesians 6:10-12

Finally, my brethren, be strong in the Lord, and in the power of his might. Put on the whole armor of God, that ye may be able to stand against the wiles of the devil. For we wrestle not against flesh and blood, but against principalities, against powers, against the rulers of the darkness of this world, against spiritual wickedness in high places.

Prayer:

Father God, each day I practice putting on the whole armor of God. Helmet of Salvation, Breastplate of righteousness, Belt of Truth, I plant my feet in preparation of peace, I have the shield of Faith and the sword of the spirit which is the Word of God. Amen   vs 10-18

Journal / Notes
Keep on my armor of God every day.

Day 6

Hebrews 11:6

But without faith it is impossible to please Him, for he who comes to God must believe that He is, and that He is a rewarder of those who diligently seek Him.

Prayer:

Father God, scripture says that you will reward me if I diligently seek you. The more I seek you Lord, the more I get to know you and it brings wisdom, revelation and knowledge. This is my reward!

Journal / Notes:

What a reward! Revelation of who God is in His Word, getting to know Him and who He is!

Day 7

2 Corinthians 4:18

While we do not look at the things which are seen, but at the things which are not seen. For the things which are seen are temporary, but the things which are not seen are eternal.

Isaiah 54:17   CEV translation

Weapons made to attack you
    won't be successful;
words spoken against you
    won't hurt at all
My servants, Jerusalem is yours!
I, the Lord, promise
    to bless you with victory.

Psalms 23:4

I may walk through valleys
as dark as death,
    but I won't be afraid.
You are with me,
and your shepherd's rod
    makes me feel safe.

1 Peter 1:5

You have faith in God, whose power will protect you until the last day. Then he will save you, just as he has always planned to do.

Ephesians 6:10-12

Finally, my brethren, be strong in the Lord, and in the power of his might.
Put on the whole armor of God, that ye may be able to stand against the wiles of the devil. For we wrestle not against flesh and blood, but against principalities, against powers, against the rulers of the darkness of this world, against spiritual wickedness in high places.

Hebrews 11:6

But without faith it is impossible to please Him, for he who comes to God must believe that He is, and that He is a rewarder of those who diligently seek Him.

This week's prayer according to the Word!

Heavenly Father, I thank you for your Word that I have sown in my heart this week, for the truth of your Word being manifested in my heart to bring forth faith. For being able to see that it is the unseen things that are eternal and that I don't have to be controlled by circumstances or obstacles. I thank you that no matter what I face I know your Word tells me that you are with me, that no weapon formed against me will prosper, that my Faith in you God and your power will protect me! You promise me in your Word that I have the victory. You give me armor that I can put on daily Ephesians 6:10-18. I diligently seek you Father God, I submit to my daily Word and Prayer knowing that you will reward me. Amen!

Made in the USA
Columbia, SC
30 November 2024

48036882R00024